Praise for *The River Only Runs One Way*
+ Mary Lou Kayser

"Mary Lou's poetry is a powerful reminder to lead with empathy and to find beauty in our journey toward self-discovery. Her work challenges us to be better, kinder, and more resilient humans, and that no matter our achievements or challenges in life, we are all connected by our shared experiences of pain, joy, and growth."
-Tommy Breedlove, Business & Leadership Coach & Keynote Speaker, USA Today & WSJ Bestselling author of *Legendary*

"This collection reflects the wisdom accumulated from human experiences like love, loss, and motherhood. Mary Lou's use of nature as the lens through which she reflects on these experiences is brilliant. She connects to the senses in a way that makes painful memories vivid, but also safe to explore as the reassuring rhythm of nature underlies each piece, smoothing out the volatility of life. I keep revisiting these poems and luxuriating in the hopefulness in which they envelop me."
-Amy Bobchek, Executive Leader & Sales Strategist

"In an era overwhelmed by constant interruptions and the incessant buzz of daily life, *The River Only Runs One Way* offers a profound sanctuary. This collection of poetry draws me away from my digital screens, guiding me instead into a serene, vibrant world where I yearn to linger. Through vivid descriptions, the poems evoke the calming sounds of birds and flowing water, inviting me into a mental space of reflection and healing. The words gently lead me to embrace my vulnerability, allowing me to explore my past, present, and future with peace. This book is a much-needed escape, a sanctuary of poems that heals and soothes."
-Chris Miller, Sales Leader & Coach

Also by Mary Lou Kayser and Kingfisher Media Publishing:

Books

The Far Unlit Unknown
Personal Branding Secrets for Beginners
If Today Was a Shape
Leadership Limericks
The Ones Who Believed

Podcast

Play Your Position

THE RIVER ONLY RUNS ONE WAY

Mary Lou Kayser

poems

NEW YORK | BEAVERTON

Kingfisher Media Publishing
8630 SW Scholls Ferry Road, #123
Beaverton, OR 97008
www.MaryLouKayser.com

Cover design: Diana Rosinus
Cover image: marvalens (licensed by Adobe Stock Images)
Interior images licensed by Adobe Stock Images

ISBN 979-8-9877923-3-9 softcover
ISBN 979-8-9877923-4-6 hardcover
ISBN 979-8-9877923-5-3 ebook

Publisher's Cataloging-In-Publication Data

Names: Kayser, Mary Lou, author.
Title: The river only runs one way : poems / Mary Lou Kayser.
Description: Beaverton, Oregon : Kingfisher Media Publishing, [2024]
Identifiers: ISBN: 979-8-9877923-3-9 (softcover) | 979-8-9877923-4-6 (hardcover) | 979-8-9877923-5-3 (ebook)
Subjects: LCSH: Rivers--Poetry. | Change--Poetry. | Life--Psychological aspects--Poetry. | Self-acceptance--Poetry. | Self-consciousness (Awareness)--Poetry. | Compassion--Poetry. | LCGFT: Poetry. | Self-help publications. | BISAC: POETRY / Subjects & Themes /Motivational & Inspirational. | POETRY / Women Authors. | SELF-HELP / Personal Growth / Self-Esteem.
Classification: LCC: PS3611.A927 R58 2024 | DDC: 811/.6--dc23

Published in the United States of America

For the rivers and the solitude,

who protect and touch and greet me

"Eventually, all things merge into one, and a river runs through it."

–NORMAN MACLEAN

"Love consists in this, that two solitudes protect and touch and greet each other."

–RAINER MARIA RILKE

Contents

Introduction

I was 20 years old when I became a rafting guide on the Kenai River in Alaska.

It's an understatement to say that the river worked its way into my bones that summer. And it's still there, decades later, a quiet force flowing in the background of my life every day, reminding me of what matters most.

I witnessed first hand what happens when the river becomes a part of you. I also witnessed that the river only runs one way.

And it doesn't stop running.

During my tenure as a river guide, I made hundreds of trips down the Kenai River. Not one of them was the same even though technically, I was passing through the same territory on the same river each time I made a run.

But with each venture, different fish were swimming upstream. The sockeye salmon arrived, and then spawned. The eagles I had seen the day before were not in the tree when I passed it the next day. The mama moose and her baby had moved on to a different place to eat river grass.

In our busy world with distractions coming at us from every direction, it's too easy to lose track of time and miss the simple things our natural world offers us. We get tangled up in things that don't matter only to reach a point when we realize how much time is gone -- and we can't get it back.

While the poems in this collection reflect several themes like love, loss, freedom, and change, the big one is the relationship we each have to the passage of time. How moments pass and we can't get them back.

Subtle changes are always going on all around us. Part of our job while we are here is to not waste our time trying to go back to something that no longer exists, but to be more aware of the moments as we live them.

Birds and trees, flowers and lakes, the call of the loon, stars and campfires and that special feeling you get when sitting next to someone you love -- each becomes a portal to new beginnings, celebrating the magic inherent to being alive in our natural world.

My wish for you as you read these poems is that you reflect upon your life including the moments that stay with you, the moments that have passed, and the moments that lie ahead.

To grant yourself grace for making decisions that didn't work out the way you thought they would. For taking risks because you were curious. For noticing what seems invisible but has been here all along. For forgiving those who hurt you along the way, as difficult as it is to do that.

And for ultimately forgiving and loving yourself for being human.

Recognizing that while Time is infinite, our time here in our physical bodies is not. Still, we can always choose to do the most with what we're given.

We can show up to each day with gratitude and humility and intentionality so that when our time is up, we can look back and say, "Yes, the river only runs one way. I made the most of what I had. And it was good."

Mary Lou Kayser
June 2024

Headwaters

"Things take the time they take. Don't worry."

–MARY OLIVER

Ghost Plant

The summer
I discovered
The ghost plant
Peaking out
From fallen leaves
Its pale bell face
Curved in prayer
Toward the ground
Its gentle neck
Like yours
Kind and contemplative

I found an owl feather
On the road
It was a sign
Whispered from the woods
Of secrets about us
Not yet told

From a great horned owl
I first believed
But would hence discover
Belonged to
A different breed
A lone barred owl
Who cooks for you
And I wondered
Who cooked for you
When I wasn't around

Did she stop by or

Was there someone else
Who knew exactly
The way you like
Your ribeye
Partly pink inside
With sautéed mushrooms
Creamed spinach
And mashed potatoes
On the side

Who brought you red wine
From small Italian vineyards
And smiled when you
Shook your head
Approving the meal
You were just fed

Who felt connected
Beyond the years
We didn't know each other
I've cried my tears
About time that's passed
When we weren't together
Like so many lost
Owl feathers

But tonight at this table
We will raise a glass
To honor the ghosts
From our respective pasts
To what is now and
Yet to unfold
Our story grows with us
As we grow old

If Something You Love Is Almost Gone

Loneliness led me to you
Neither of us was looking
And yet —
There
In the dark
We were finally home

I want to know everything
About you
Explore every inch of
Your skin
Hear every story in
Your mind
Taste every salty drop from
Your kind
And yet —

I never want to be so familiar
As to never want you again
Pulse inside me
Swallow my heart
Make me laugh and cry
And sigh and groan

Maybe loneliness can keep
Things at bay
We can stay in the new
The way I dream about you
Wearing emerald green
And your hair is still long

If something you love
Is almost gone —
Evaporating rain

Will Loneliness once again
Lead us home?

No Name for This

There is no name for this

A look
That glance
The feeling of sitting
On a couch and
The air smells
A certain way

A blend of the candle
On the mantel
Called "Mountain"
And hot laundry
Fresh from the dryer
A hint of
Tobacco deodorant
Spicy cologne
Morning turning
Into afternoon
And now --
Evening on a cold
November night

The light on the dash
That one song
Always comes on
Dinner
At a favorite restaurant
The first taste
Of Tanqueray and tonic
When it hits the tongue

Brushed denim
A silky cream blouse

Laughing all the way
Back to the house

How could one word
Possibly express
What this is -- so no

There is no name for this

Maybe in a Day

Maybe in a day
I can remove myself
from the spaciousness
of wanting another more
than I want myself

To look at
the bark of a tree
up close and
run my hands
over its rough trunk
without thinking about
how good it felt
when rough hands
ran over me

Maybe in a day
the rain will move
out to sea
clearing the sky and
the debris left behind
on my shore
broken shells have
their own kind
of beauty and
they say sunlight
disinfects everything

I have smiled
on cloudless mornings
head tilted toward the sun
bright with possibility
and birds
doing their thing

Maybe in a day
I won't remember
what that first
sip of wine tasted like
from the bottle
carried across the miles
far away or
those eyes
close across the table
shining with their own
version of the sunrise

You know the kind —

So much color expanding
in your heart
brings you to your knees
and you cry
because nothing
is more alive
in that moment
than your tears reflecting
the sun rising
in those eyes

This Is My Face

This is my face
Imperfect in many ways
Asymmetrical in others
Which makes me
Different and beautiful
In every way

When I smile
My nose broadens and
I see my mother

One eye looks
Smaller than the other

When I laugh
My dad's
Crinkles appear
On either side
Of my eyes

Grooves next
To my mouth
Are solely my own
Roads of the world
I've traveled and where
I have laughed and
I have loved and
I have lived

Stories in the scars
Beneath one eyebrow
From the time I fell
When I believed
I could fly

Apple cheeks
Where heat will rise
When loved ones kiss
Side to side
And lips that kiss
Ones I love
Hello and goodbye

This is my face and
I don't miss
The way it once was
Or try to freeze it
In some other time
I love what it is and
Who I am because
It is one hundred percent
Mine

Rabbits Doing Rabbit Things

This is the work:

I love a way that
No longer exists

Not like rabbits
Doing rabbit things

Love like humans
Doing human things

Mucking it up
Because we can

Dragging with us
Chains of potential

Because who
Doesn't love

The heavy sweetness
Of potential

What we carry
Into the beginning

Doesn't last
Can't last

The script shifts
Or maybe the lies

Were always there
Promises implied

Swallowed by
Our imagination

Deaf to what's said
Between the lines

Scene follows scene
Cut to the chase

Rabbits doing
Rabbit things

Remembering what
We won't erase

Falling for it
Every time

Source

after a while
it all begins
to sound the same
first light
waves goodbye
to midnight
two cardinals
saddle up
to the seeds
squirrels chase
each other
up and down
the grand oak tree

the day launches
into a rush of
hashtags and headlines
reconstructed
from yesterday's news
how many times
do you need
to be reminded
what doesn't kill you
makes you stronger

each sentence
each word
builds upon an idea
a thought
someone else's dream
somewhere else
some other time
long before
you came along

to drink
from the river
of what could be

you seek not a life
from their imagination
but one you construct
on the trail you follow
toward your source
where a completely
different story
has yet to leave
its footprints

every river begins
somewhere
tender and small
with nothing
but the desire
to move
in the direction
of the sea
guiding it forward
of its own free will
and there
the water
bubbles clearest
and cold
in your mouth
untainted
most pure

When Someone Famous Dies

When someone famous dies
we like to think
we knew them
or at least
something about them,
perhaps more than
what was true.

We look
at their Instagram
for clues.

Was their death predicted?

Did they know?

We like to think
they were our friend.
But the truth is,
we didn't know them.

Not really.

We didn't know
the demons
they faced
each day or
the depth of
their struggle.

We didn't understand
what it was like
to be them.

We projected
the movie reel of
our own hopes
and dreams,
desires and wants,
onto the slender sliver
of their silver screen,
living vicariously
through the lens
of their life.

Forgetting sometimes
that like us,
they had to
feel the ground
beneath their
own feet
each day.
Like us, their job
was to keep
shining their light and
moving forward, too.

We cannot let
the death of
someone famous
stop us from
moving forward and
shining our light.

We can pause
and collectively grieve.

We can remember
their smile and
the way they
made us laugh.

In the wake
of losing someone
we felt we knew
we can only hope that
we double down
on our own futures and
become even more
aware of who we are
right now and
who we are
meant to become.

for Matthew Perry

Love Letter to Myself, no.3

The crazy thing is
We still need each other
Forget self-reliance for a minute
And boot straps
And independence

Zoom in on
What's really going on

The buzz up your spine
From a stranger's smile
The sound of people
Laughing so hard
Your food gets cold
And cheeks glow wild
With embers of life

Life!

What a concept
To want to live
Among the ruins
To want to hear
An acoustic guitar and
Witness clouds expanding
On the wild edge
Of growing rain
And smell his clothes
At the end of a day
And the trail of perfume
Lingering down the hall

To crave that first taste
Of hot and spicy and

The surprising softness
Of an elephant's trunk
Snuffling peanuts
From your hand
At the circus
When you were eight

This is what it means to be alive!

Forget for a minute
The spin cycle
Of violence and hate
Step through this garden gate
Of infinite spring
Splendor and jazz
Reminding us
We still need each other
And oh most definitely!

More life awaits

This Song I Sing of Men

This song I sing of men
Is not just for
The busted pipes
Or preparing the power boat
For the summer
Processing wood
Fixing a bad breaker
Rebooting the cable box
Filling holes in the drywall
Or when the kitchen floods

This song I sing of men
Is as ancient as the dirt
On their hands and under
Their fingernails
Permanent ink marking
Their commitment to
The monumental width
Of their shoulders and
What they carry in their arms
And on their backs
And the ache in their feet
At the end of a long, long day

Men oh men we need you
More than ever
This independence thing and
I can do it all myself
Grew old and stale
A long time ago

I'm worn down
Worn out
Bone weary

Done in
Done for

Tired

I want a man by my side
Hard and tender
Kind and unwilling to back down
A lover and companion
Who knows who he is
And shows up to help
Who makes no apologies for being
Fully one hundred percent himself

Who curses what's wrong
And stands up for what's right
Who works hard and
Who admits when he's tired, too
Steps forward even when
He doesn't feel like it
Because sometimes
We just don't feel like it
But we do it anyway
Because it's the right thing to do

I want a man whose kisses are soft
And hugs me hard
Who respects women
For the work we do
And loves me for being a woman
And values me for who I am
Beyond being a woman
And how hard I work, too

Because we all work hard
We do
With dirt on our hands

And the ache in our feet
Because we are all worn down
We are all
Worn out
Bone weary
Done in
Done for

Tired

And we need each other
We need to sing
With and to each other
Carry each other
More than ever
We need each other
The width of our shoulders
We do

Hold Fast the Kayak

Hold fast the kayak
On northern blue
The space between
Is calling you

The space between
Then and there
Where Winters bet on
Summers fair

Where edges rough
And tumble trees of
Grandeur sinks you
To your knees

A sharp reminder
The sun shines now
Hold fast the kayak
Heart place, soul sound

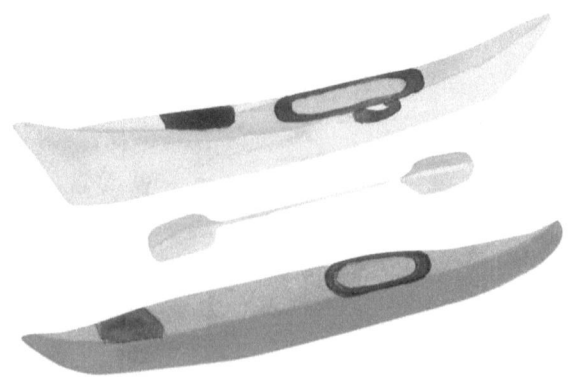

Van Gogh's Stars or Love Letter to Myself, no. 6

August night
On the dock
Under Van Gogh's stars
Stars and stars and
So many stars
In a grand expanse
Of thick inky darkness
One shoots
Then a second
Trailing through infinity
Vast and true
I imagine his hand
Reaching for mine
Across that vast expanse
A meteor between us
The length of states
The width of the universe
The weight of time
And I feel it
His hand in mine
In that darkness
His dark eyes glowing
Leading me home
As more stars
Give light
Shine fast
Sublime

Arsenal

Some people
Want you to believe
Love is not enough

It doesn't
Heal all wounds

It doesn't
Promise you
The moon

Or make someone
Love you, too

But to reach for
Anything else
Inside the arsenal

Even when
You don't get

Love back
The way maybe
You thought you would

Is a fool's errand
A zero sum game

Perpetuating a terrible lie
Because the truth —
The Truth about love

Love gives of itself
Every single time

Without conditions
Or restrictions
Or manipulations
Or questions
You are love

And that alone
Is enough
It's enough

saudade

I feel like I'm just starting
This business called loneliness
This never ending longing
For someone who doesn't exist
A figment of my imagination, yes
And thus so very real
Only he does not — cannot — manifest

Rendering no post with #blessed
No matter how much I think
He will one day show up and say
Hello, darling. Fall into my arms
And rest your tired soul
And your ragged heart
On my chest

I will hold you as long
As you need me
And when I leave
It won't be goodbye
You won't have to cry
Yourself to sleep

Because I'm here, darling
Your presence
My silence
Our absence just starting

Let us be less lonely like clouds
And more friendly like sunflowers
Bowing toward the sun
In one grand gesture of
Gratitude and forgiveness

Sitting with You in Stillness

There's a place
Under the stars
Among the trees
That smells like

New dirt and leaves
Sitting with you there
In stillness we have
No need for words

The sound of wind
An owl calling
Coyotes yipping
And our breathing

Two hearts aligned
One world found
Souls side by side
A place worth keeping

Clearly

My house is not clean
Smudges smeared across the
Refrigerator door
Dust on every baseboard
And all over the blinds
Laundry piled high
Dishes too
And the leaves
In the driveway
Have turned into
Orange Peaks
Too high to climb

But today
I have a new poem with
Gleaming edges and
Folded lines and
I can see clearly
Through the windows
Of its words
Where I find
Peace in the fragments
And raw glorious vistas
Of my wild thoughts and
Chaotic mind

Love Is Like That

Here and then gone
But never forever

No

Love is like that

Love is the sunset
Saying good night
To the day

Love is a bee
Pollinating trees

Love is the wind
Pushing waves
Crashing against the shore

Crashing inside your heart
Love is like that

Wild from the start

I Always Looked So Pretty in His House

I always looked so pretty in his house
On the couch the light caught
The green flecks in my eyes
The ones he liked when I rimmed
Them with gold on fancy nights

I noticed him noticing my eyes
After he noticed my tits and ass
I didn't mind things went in that order
I liked his hands on me in
The Levis he liked low on my hips

I liked his eyes on my tits
Whenever I wore a silky blouse
Or a white tee shirt
When my nipples got hard
My hands shook like my body

Under his and when he asked
I took photos and sent them to him
Hard beneath my shirt to keep
In his secret vault next to the ones
Of me naked on the bed before I knew

Looking pretty in his house
Wouldn't, no -- it couldn't last

Burning the Words

The letter I wrote
Would not ignite
When I wanted it
To burn

I stood on the dock
And could not
Get the flame
To catch

Wind at my back
I sheltered the match
Curled into myself
The task

But alas — the wind
Was too strong
So I tore the paper into
Shreds instead

And said his name
As if he could hear
We're not done, not yet
That's clear

To not burn the letter
I wrote you means the
We as I've known us
Is still here

I Don't Know Who Needs to Hear This Today

You are beautiful
And worthy of love

You have been enough
Since the day

You were born
You matter to the world

Because you are here now
A bright and tender light

Guiding us through
Our darkness

Confluence

"We are dealing in a magic realm.

Nobody knows why or how it works."

–RICK RUBIN

Delta

The question isn't
will they change

the question is
do you want them

in your life
exactly as they are

Rewilding

Change is the nature of life
Returning to the land
what we used
is our greatest gesture
A triumph of rewilding
That we once needed and now —
No longer call home

All we can do is our best
Receive the seasons
Honor the cycles
Bear witness to what is
Let go of what once was
Embrace our solitude
And trust in the next journey
New joys will open to us

We will continue
We will love
We will live

Extending the Line

I wanted you
To be my third love
The one they say
Comes after the first
And heartbreak and
Figuring myself out

I wanted you
To look at me
The way my dad
Looked at my mom
From across the room
His One True Love

I wanted you
To choose a song
We would sing out loud
Driving down the road
In the early dark
Anchored to the cords

I wanted you
To sever your past
Beyond the pain
Abandoned for good
Because my arrival
Allowed you to let go

I wanted you
To carry me forever
Across the threshold
Into the bed we chose

Together where we found
Each other for good

I wanted you
        I wanted you
                I wanted you

Extending the line
                Extending the line
                        Extending the line

The Right and Resting Place

This house
Is not your house
You are passing through

This place
Once of it
Now, not so

You pass the statue where
Once you waited
For a boy

Who never showed
Who made promises
You then could not keep

Each day a visitor
Heading elsewhere
You rest at night and

Wake refreshed and
Restless for what
New promises teach

What promises
Are you making
To yourself now

To where
You will go next
What place will whisper,

Here is where
You belong

Never there
You knew when
You were young

And now, flooded
With twilight
You know different things

About the stars
Shining on the inside
Where once it was dark

And you could not see
What is clear and bright
On the path

In the right and
Resting place
Revealing all you had

The Unknowing

On this side of unknowing
I answer your call anyway
Habit I suppose and
Something else
I've felt
From our first collision

Two falling stars
Brushing up against
Each other
The best kind of night sky
Abundant and uncharted

What might we still see
Sends a thrill through me
The same thrill I feel
When our arms rest
Against each other and
I feel the warmth of your skin

When you tell me a story
Your eyes finding mine
From across the table
Beyond the bottle of wine
We share with a meal

In those moments
Our light shines
Through the impossible darkness
Of our lives
Confirming how much I love
Being together
And alone

And how the unknowing
Makes it so

Arrival

You always meet the new you
in the form of a stranger

Twenty

on a twenty minute walk
without your phone
you will find
yourself waiting
on that path
for a deeper conversation

What Small Hands

Ran their fingers
Across the stitching on
Another pair of jeans
You don't need

What small hands
Gathered the hem
Smoothed down the pockets
Slid along the placket

Stuck their calloused thumbs
Through button holes
Barely wide enough
For new dreams

Chafed and raw
What small hands
Carried another bolt of
Denim through air thick

With loose fibers
Tangled knots of
Forget about leaving —
you're never

Going anywhere
No reason to wonder
If these jeans fit (they don't)
Or if they make

Your ass look fat
What small hands
Are busy elsewhere and
Aren't made for that

The Roof Outside My Window

The roof outside
My window
Used to be red
Where I snuck out
At night, then in

Where boys climbed
The pussywillow tree
And howled
Where I sat with friends
Smoking Marlboros

Packed tight against
Slender wrists
Where I talked philosophy
And soccer players long
Into the afternoon

With the boy I longed
To kiss, who secretly
Howled for me, too
And grew up to be
A lawyer with two kids

Now it's shingled black
And the house that
Once was white
Is the color of milky tea
Latte love with

Matcha trim, peeling in all
The obvious places, secretly

Longing for conversation
And unmet expectations
To howl again

Two Words

Together
We made a world
You + I
We + Us
Two distinct voices
One uncommon love

A bridge between then
And tomorrow
We showed up for now
Combined independence
Two words we're made of

I Forgot How Much I Love September

I forgot how much I love September
And how good you look in faded jeans
The way the light hangs low in the sky
How nothing I think is what it seems

I forgot how much I love the water
And how good it feels on autumn skin
The way the moon barely kisses stars
How when I show up you let me in

I forgot how much I love not knowing
When you'll leave and come back again
The way you look walking out the door
How your lips brush mine leading up til then

I forgot how much I love September
And the way you smile after being gone
How my love for you grows ever stronger
The way you never forget a favorite song

That Hard Way

Will you go
That hard way with me
Turn toward the storm
With icy wind and cruel rain
Tearing at our skin

Will you hold
My hand as lightning
Rips apart the sky
Shredding clouds
Splintering trees

Will you and I emerge
From the fire
With our hearts still intact
Love unruptured
Upon impact

Will we each be
One of the few who agree
Despite the sharp edges
My darling, yes
You can count on me

Even More Than You Already Do

To bring another
Into your life
Make room and
Space for conversation
Dirty laundry
More dishes in the sink

Requires effort and
Fortitude you can find
If you want to
If having another in
Your life matters
You have the room

You can throw wide
The windows
Invite light to come in
Open that bottle of wine
The one you've been saving
For this kind of occasion

Space is always available
It does the heart good
When laughter fills
The halls where loneliness
Has wandered far too long
On tired aching feet

It's not forever
Nothing ever is
And for now, here,
Another softens the sadness
And you forget how heavy
Your anguish and the sorrow

A Recent Study

When compared to being alone
to being with you

Statistically
Mathematically
Empirically
Instinctively

I can confidently conclude

I am fundamentally happier alone and
      wildly, ecstatically, ferociously, pleasantly
           so very surprisingly content with you

Direction

To find our way
Through the woods

We need to show
Each other our maps

Break branches
For breadcrumbs

And hand over
Our flashlight

And not assume
We already

Understand how
Any of it works

shooting star

i was here and
you were here
and together
we made a world

By the Lake

All is not quiet and calm
By the lake tonight

Waves roar against the shore
Smashing hard the rocks

Nymphs die in the jaws of fish
No stars shine in a stormy sky

Ferocious water and wind
Carry the call of the loon

That mournful and haunting sound
Chilling the bones

Awakening what's buried and
Not forgotten deep in your heart

Where grief and mourning live
Torturing your wild fractured mind

When you dare to step outside
All is not clear and you admit

You're blind from the longing
With no taste for the haunting —

He's gone
He's gone
He's gone

Finding the Words

I don't think it's possible
To find the words
For how it feels
After he leaves for good
Like rocks along the shore
Or when you see
Birds flying in a V

They aren't as easy
To uncover from wicked dirt
Packed hard and dark
Around the fence where
He stole a kiss and
Promised not to hide
What you felt inside

You held that kiss like a
Crown of thorns and
Didn't mind the blood or
When you were late
One night he waited
And you didn't come
It's okay, he said

We always have tomorrow
And you didn't have
The courage to say he lied
No matter how hard you tried
How could you find the words
To say tomorrow isn't promised
Not for him, anyway

Not for any of us but he
Didn't think that way as if

Time is a predetermined
Variable doled out fairly
By unknown standards and
Extravagant gestures
Honored and respected rarely

Especially when it seems
It's on your side and
It will be there all along
A simple question to find the words
For the way of love and for
The asking of it, buried deep in
The red winged blackbirds' song

Always the Words

The year his father died
I took his writing class
It was summer on the fertile campus
There among the trees

Beyond the library a courtyard
Where you can witness mountains
And throw coins into a fountain
A testament to giants
Like we all aspired to be

In his father's image
(or footsteps, at least)
He brought to us his own ways
Of seeing the world

Through words (always the words)
I listened, in awe of the man
Who had made him, humbled by the man
Who had guided him as he
In turn, guided us

Together we remembered our fathers
And wrote to them as only children can
Wanting to please the ones
Who made us real through flesh and love

And then -- through words we said
Amen in one long final breath
A testament to what is and had been
And then -- always, always the words

for Kim Stafford

Rapids

"This is the story of how we begin to remember."

—PAUL SIMON

In the Waiting Area at the Alfond Center

A display on the wall
Tells me Harold Alfond
Was a champion for Maine.
A woman waiting with me says
"Enjoy the next few days of sun.
It will all be gone way too soon."

My mother emerges from the lab
The badge of blood drawn
Taped to her arm. She knows
Where to go next. Downstairs
Lower Level she pushes double ells
on the Elevator button.

I find a chair next to the window.
Mom notices the empty corner
And laments the missing round table
She remembers offered visitors
a jigsaw puzzle to make waiting more tolerable
Another casualty of Covid

A nurse in blue scrubs calls mom's name
She wheels herself through the single door
and disappears down a hall as
A man and his daughter emerge
Followed by a different nurse

She's wearing a green jumpsuit with
Brown Dansko clogs.
"We are going to go upstairs and get you an XRay,"
she says in a voice too loud for inside.

"After that your daughter will take you to the hospital
For a CT of your chest and your pelvis."
He says nothing, as if he's already accepted his fate.

What will the X-ray show or
do they already know?
This is a place that knows things
Sometimes before their time
Like my dad who didn't let on
What he knew, claiming he was fine

It's arthritis, he'd say. I'm also 83.
What did he know he wouldn't tell mom or me?
We'll never know.
He won't walk through a door down a hallway
to get his blood drawn.
He won't return with a bloody cotton ball
wedged in the crux of his arm
announcing all is well.
He's gone now, and so is his smile,
too soon before his time.

The Darling

What's different
Draws us together
What's different
Tears us apart

Pulled toward
Each other
Too close
Our tender hearts

We snarl
Blood mouths
We gnash
Broken teeth

We punch
Gnarled fists
We explode
Rough heat

What's different
Opens our souls
What's different
Shuts us down

What's different
Closes the holes
What's different
Carries the sound

We laugh
Wide tongues
We cry
Full eyes

We hold
Weathered hands
We sleep
Side by side

What's different
Doesn't matter
What's different
Let's us know

What's different
Is the darling
What's different
Loves us so

Hurricane Season

I own
the decision
to step through
your door
and stick around
despite the
storm brewing
on the horizon

Doing your dishes
and folding
your laundry
watching the sky
turn from blue
to gray

I choose to stay
despite knowing
one day
you will leave
We all leave
one day

And so
the question
becomes

Do I move
through
the pain
now

And say
goodbye or

do I stay
knowing the pain
is heading
my way

As predictable
as hurricane season
the storm
building on
the horizon
and as likely
as spring rain

Low Tide

I could sit here and lie and
Say the meanness doesn't hurt
Pretend

The cruelty is merely a shot
Over the bow of a culture
We created

In the name of what?

Certainty not love

Love doesn't look like
Shoving and shouting, all caps
On an anonymous keyboard
Or in a text

I'm done trying to figure out
When the tide of decency turned

Or has it always been this low and
I chose not to see the broken shells of
Greed and self-loathing scattered
across the country's floor

Even rising tides from climate change
Won't hide what's there, lurking
Along the edges of our worn out souls

Starving for someone else to solve
The mess we have made
The mess we refuse to clean up

Let it be someone else's problem or fault
Too much else to do, after all

In the name of what?

What will it take, I wonder
To agree about decisions for the future
To not be lazy today

To think about not only ourselves
But the ones who are too small
To know any different or better

Who watch what we do and swear
In tiny voices only they can hear:
Not me. I won't do that, too

I cannot sit by and lie
And tell myself
Or anyone else
Any of this is okay
Because it's not
Not even a little bit
Not now, not then

And not when
We congratulate ourselves
For figuring out
A new answer
To a different problem
Or lose the weight
Pay off the mortgage
Make more money
Any excuse will do

It may already be too late

As for the Children

Not yet.

I'm not ready.

Not because
when I first learned
about you
I was afraid.

Afraid of doing it wrong.

Afraid of not hugging or
loving you enough.

Afraid of being
swallowed alive
by your purity
and those eyes.

Your chubby arms
and chubbier legs.

Bread dough of my soul.

I couldn't get enough
of rolling you
through my heart and
with my hands
and the tug on my breasts
long after I was empty.

The smell
of the top
of your head.

It didn't matter when
they tore you out of me
because you didn't want to leave
the kindness of
that warm sheltered embrace
tucked so far up under my rib cage
I could barely breathe.

I didn't mind.

I liked you there and
I was also relieved
after you arrived.

For the first time
I understood
love at first sight and
what it means
to catch your breath.

Outside of me
you were you
immediately.

I could see that, clearly.

And now —

Still so much like the first time
we held each other's gaze
only better for the years of forging
in the fire your one wild
and precious life,
what it means to be alive and
who you are.

I knew in that moment

I'd never be the same
and how happy I was knowing
you would make me that way.

How could anyone after that
be ready for the day you leave?
I'll never be ready
(how can anyone ever be ready!)

Because leaving —

Oh wretched, monstrous, destroy my heart leaving —

Is the only thing any of us
is guaranteed.

And I'm not ready.

Not yet.

I don't think
I'll ever be.

Misunderstanding

Maybe some things
Don't make sense
By their essence
They are not meant
To be understood

By their nature
They exist in
Eternal difference
Mismatched
Divided

So separate from
Your Self
Your best bet is
To stand still
In wonder gazing

At their impossible
Immutable magnificence

Today Might Be a Hard Day

Today might be a hard day.
A day you cry hard for a long time.
All the grief you've kept inside
has had enough and says, *Fuck this*,
pouring out of you in a torrent of tears.

You cry so hard your head hurts.
Your eyes are swollen and you wonder
if you will ever feel joy or laugh again.
You honestly can't answer that question.

You feel hopeless and helpless and worthless.
You're having bad thoughts that scare you
so you call the number. Ya, *that* number.
You talk to a kind woman named Linda
who understands the depth of your ache
for mountains and forests and rivers
running cold and deep. She helps you
back from the edge of permanent nothing.

Later you take a selfie to document
the hard days, too, if only to remind yourself
that it's not always easy, but it is always worth it.
Growth hurts. You notice your face looks
more relaxed in the photo, raccoon eyes aside.
You also notice your bicep is more defined.
And you think, *Okay. Evidence of progress.*
You are growing and it's good even if it hurts.
Evidence that there is hope and tomorrow
won't be so hard.

The Heart Always Knows

The thing is
You will never know

Not the way you want to know
This is certain

You will be safe
And your heart won't break

The heart always knows
It can break and still it grows

The trees in a storm don't know
Which among them will fall

Which one will be ripped from
The earth as the wind howls and rages

Trees don't try to hold on
When it's time

They surrender
And in their final moments

You want to believe they knew
Their life mattered

They were grateful for the power
Of their trunks and their branches

Providing shelter and a place
To nest and rest

It's safe to say you can know
These things, too

Even if you can never know
Which storm will uproot you

It will always be okay to offer
Your shelter to another

Among your leaves and branches
Your eyes and smile and embrace

May just be the safety they seek
On this weary leg of their journey

When their strength returns
And the time comes to fly

You will remember the clouds part
For the endless rush of sky

And you can
give your heart away

And it will come back
Because even if you don't know

Your heart does
Because the heart always knows

Rapids

What do you do
to your continual astonishment?

In what bountiful ways
do you amaze yourself?

How do you celebrate
all your weird wonderfulness?

How fast are you running
towards your wildest dreams?

The Great Unfolding

we could all use more
of the great unfolding
into the wondrous mess of life
and a whole lot less
of the tiresome withdrawal
into a perfectly filtered death

Forecast

Some storms come
Not to destroy your life
But to clear the path
Towards deeper understanding

Making the Turn

Give me
the eye wall
any day
I'll take
its blistering
winds and
devastating rain
over the
unpredictable turn
a Hurricane
can take
deceptive
and cruel
on its path
of intentions
until it's too late

The Source of My Aggression

This is not new
The white hot flames of
Knowledge and
Awareness

Inciting self-hatred
Blisters of rage
The shape of my fists
In your face and
In mine

Bruised
Doesn't describe
How hard the hurt

Broken
Doesn't extend
Any consolation

Bloody
Doesn't grant justice
To what's torn inside

Incite
      Insight
Inside

Where curled and raw
I move anyway and ask:

Break my collarbone
Shoot me
Stab me

Punch me down
    And down
        And down

The curve of your back
A bottle rocket
Arcs into shoulders
Sparks spiral
Toward anything

Sparks

Cracking

    Twisting

        Writhing

            Flailing

Because to stay

Coiled
Unexpressed
Silent
Still

The firing line

BOOM
-- and it's gone

Signs of My Disconnection

Why do we stubbornly
Work ourselves up
Chasing the many
When in the end
We are known
To so few

And Then What

After the money comes in
And the diagnosis
The hard conversation
The next steps and prognosis —

What happens when
And then what
Has no answer
Nothing's definitive or clear

You hear only that
Which fits inside the container
That's always been there
The same one you've carried
All these years —

The ring
The jar
The purse
The car
The crash
The burn
The rise
The turn
The smoke
The drink
The bed
The sink
The house
The job
The love
The fear

And then what
And then what
And then what, my dear?

A Different Kind of Trauma

We give our lives
To those we love
Necessity knocks and
We open the door

Our dreams can wait
When shadows call
Generations of yes
To the chain and ball

Heartbreak's familiar
Crushing pain of
Empty pockets and
Low beat same

Bleary weary
Dusty shelves
Lies we believe
And tell ourselves

Throwing Stars

This is the crisis
    Sharp edges

Mitigate threats
    Don't get too close

Please come closer
    Side by side

The gulf between us
    Unbearably wide

I want you
    Me too but

We is a four letter word
    Scarred and untethered

Throwing stars
    At our hearts

Is easier than
    The other so

Why not pierce
    The soul instead

Rugged Rescue

You want it so much
you'll do ANYTHING

Won't you?

Can you honestly
say this to yourself
about what you're
(probably half-assedly)
pursuing?

Like.

Seriously.

Look yourself in the eye
without immediately looking away
and say this out loud
with unwavering BELIEF

Stalwart CONVICTION

NOT FUCKING AROUND THIS TIME

As if
it is
your bonafide
TRUTH

As if
it is
GUARANTEED

You want it so much
you'll do ANYTHING

If you blink —
if you notice
a dent
in the Universe
A scratch
through the glass
A pillow mark
on your cheek

If you look away
for even a millisecond

the answer is
a hands down
100 percent
Not gonna happen
Not even a little bit

NO.

So no.

You don't want *it*
badly enough.

You don't *want* it
badly enough.

You *don't* want it
badly enough.

You
probably
never

did
and
you
probably
never
will.

Best to admit that now
before chasing
more ghosts of what
could have been

Best to admit
you're just playing
a game with yourself
and all your friends
you've bragged to
about your Big Plans.

Your Big Dreams.

Someday...

Before sinking back
into the flat suds
of your microbrew
and opening Instagram
to see if anyone
has posted anything
remotely interesting and new

Who are you kidding anyway?

There's not a fucking thing
on Instagram
or LinkedIn
or Facebook

that's going to change your life
the way you think it might

possibly

maybe

if the moon aligns
with your astrological birth chart
and the rain doesn't come
until late Saturday night
and that one Influencer
you tagged in a post
likes what you wrote —

Not gonna happen

Not now

Not in the microbrewery

Not at 2:43 in the morning
staring into that
tiny blue screen of death

searching
scrolling
searching

for a life ring
a buoy
a rugged rescue
with thick arms
kind hands
and a neat beard
the kind he spends
time grooming

with creams that
smell like pipe tobacco
new wood
and fresh cut dreams

Anything to grasp
in the wicked waves
of unmet expectations
rolling you around
carrying you nowhere
capsized and unbound

Audience

In a room full of strangers
Expectation hangs heavy
Like a poem about to drop

Together we hold our breath
Waiting for The One to take
Their place on the single red dot

Designated (tonight anyway)
With powers beyond the group
We are mere mortals on a

Frequency so low it's impossible
To hear, let alone know the
Depth of our heartbreak or

The reach of our despair for
What could've been but was
Never there

Beast

we must learn
to discipline
our disappointment
lest it
swallow us whole
in one ugly,
monstrous,
soul crushing
gulp

a loss that has no name

look hard into the darkness
for what used to be
a loss that has no name
hiding there under the forsythia

with your favorite pink blanket
and menagerie of stuffed animals
guarding the castle of your tender heart
there, where you felt sheltered

beyond the obvious
beyond what turns out
was most sacred and beautiful
or when you found

solace on Sundays
behind the couch
in the fireside room
wrapped in pleats

of faded polyester curtains
filled with the dust of ages
and secrets old men
wearing black rimmed glasses

and short sleeved white shirts
told each other when they
met after church
or when, tucked under the folds

of your mother's skirt
you witnessed the world
without wondering

if it would not at times be cruel

when you look hard
in that darkness for
a loss that has no name
you will find a way forward

a fissure of light
so tiny and young
you cannot not see it
you cannot —

you will not —
miss it

Side Effects

Breathing will feel
Like shards of glass

Tearing out your throat
Dissecting your heart

Falling apart
Every limb

Watch each one go
Rocks thrown violently

Down below
No mercy here

Nothing will prepare you
For tumbling down

The jagged edge of
Loving someone

That hard

The Content of Our Lives

Displayed
One pixel
At a time

Splayed
Like blood stains
Across the evening
News

Another crash
A bridge collapsed
A fire destroyed

The hillside
Where people and
Animals lived
War stealing

Children
And their moms
Fathers killed

Political pawns
All this content
Sandwiched between
Another drug

This one
(Like all the others)
To slow

The tug
Toward death

The inevitable ending
We are all

Guaranteed
The content of
Our lives

Hashtagged
Spread thin
Ashes over ice
In an unforgiving sea

Of relentless
propaganda
And eternal misery

The two deep countries of your eyes

I have traveled there without a map or guide
Gazed at snow-capped mountains
Stood on the edge of vistas so vast and wide —
I believed I could see forever

Ah, Forever!

That sweet delicate lie I tell
Every time I find myself staring
Across Love's great new divide

If only I could satiate my desire
Lying at the mountain's base alongside
Can we stay like this a little longer
Limbs and tongues entwined
The lush river valley of what's yours and mine
Linger in the alpine taste of the canyon's glow
Unpretentious and sublime

Oh those mountains call me and I must go
I must climb the peaks of the two deep countries
Of your eyes
Make my way through the trees
Scramble over boulders
Ascend the ledge of what could be —
If only you'd let me
One more time

in the long loneliness to come

in the long loneliness to come
I will remember
what you feel like
in your truck
shotgun
on your couch
on top of me
inside your tent
the sounds you make
deep from dreams
when we sleep
in your bed
and when you said
everything and nothing
your voice deep rich
a gravel bed of hope
for another day
you would tell me
what you saw
on the road
and at work and
I would write
the words
that wouldn't matter if
you saw them and
they forever
went unread

Mouth

"You can never in this world love anyone you love enough."

–MARGARET WISE BROWN

The Great Release

Here's the thing:

Sometimes I don't want
A clear mind
The road less traveled
To be tuned in to
The highest frequency

Sometimes I welcome
The distractions
The busyness
The noise and
The mess
Life serves up on
A hot, hot plate

Let me burn my fingers
Touching what
I shouldn't touch
Let me feel rain
Sting my cheeks and
Chill my bones
Because I went outside
Without a coat
My clothes soaked until
My body shakes

Let me howl tears
Of rage and longing
Into the night not silent
But teeming with
The sounds of lives
I never see but hear
When lying awake

Outside my window is
The great beyond
Where everything I still
Have yet to learn awaits
One decision is all it takes
To move from this place
To another where sometimes
Seeds of unknowing
Take root and sometimes
The birds get the seeds

I'll gladly watch a hawk
Carry my seeds
In its beak and
Clutch my heart
In its talons soaring
Toward an unfamiliar place
With a view it already knows

I'll revel in seeing it
Rip apart everything
I think I believe
The great sweet release
And let me begin again

On the Day the Queen Died

On the day the Queen died
I swam to the buoy twice
And dove deep to where
Springs feed the lake
The deeper I swam,
The colder it became
A red headed woodpecker
Visited the lone oak among the pines
And I took pictures of the sun
In a painted blue sky

Chipmunks and squirrels
Scurried through the woods,
Gathering acorns and digging holes
Sensing fall's imminent arrival
Crows gathered on the road
And a loon flapped its wings on the water
Letting the cormorants know
Who reigns supreme

On the day the Queen died
I saw a porcupine splayed on pavement
Its quills erect in that barbarian way
The air was soft and warm
With barely a breeze
I thought about her devotion
To duty and service
How she learned the mechanics of trucks,
What to do when something breaks
And it was hard not to notice I am
Not a Queen

I will never look at an engine and understand
How to fix what doesn't work

I won't enjoy 73 years with my prince
I will never know what it's like to lead a nation
To accept my role as Royal and declare
For the entire world to hear and see

That I will dedicate my life
To representing an entire population
Who depend on me
Keeping their best interests at heart
Always above my own
With determination and grace
And a smile on my face
The ultimate sacrifice to duty
Surrendering my life to
The sovereignty of the crown
Knowing the throne and the throne alone
Is my one and only place

Spring Cleaning

there are brief moments
in your life
when all your heartache
makes sense
when you throw wide
the windows
after a dark and
particularly cold winter
and the smell of spring
fills the rooms and
wind from the west
wipes clean
old love's dust
and you remember
the tiny purple flowers
growing along the edges
of the porch and how
the forsythia
is so happy
to bloom first
before the tulips and
the daffodils and
even the crocuses
that come later and
crowd the scene
how easy to forget
those tiny purple flowers
and you won't
let yourself be last
not now
not ever again

Pep Talk

You are the common denominator
Of your life
Don't think for a second
Other factors are in play
Or random variables count
The way you do when
Solving for x

Nothing random about
Multiplication and division
You can move a decimal point
Measure a decision's weight
Bet on the odds of
Your success
Fulfillment
Satisfaction
Mind-set

They won't change the answer

Regardless of circumstance
The equation is 100 percent
Absolutely, algorithmically
On you
Of you
By you

It's in the proof, Dude —
One plus one
No matter what
Will always equal two

Loneliness Is a Compass

I

Loneliness is a compass
Guiding you toward becoming more
Of who you've always been
And already are and most importantly
Are meant to be

What's the simplest thing you can do
With those moments of aloneness
In the house of yourself?

Practice being alone
Build your stamina for letting people go
Including yourself because you must
Leave yourself to be yourself and
Stop speaking and listen
To old memories
They will help you enter
A new conversation

And yes — some voices will hurt
Many of them will be hard to hear

Listen anyway
They will fade as you move
Away from the shore to step once again
Into the river of your life

It never stopped flowing
Even though you thought it did

II

The past as you know it is about to end
And your understanding of the past
Is about to change

What you think you knew about your father
What you remember thinking about your mother
What you once understood about yourself
And everyone you've ever loved—

Don't be afraid to pick up the broom and
Sweep away musty memories
Lingering too long inside the closet
Of secrets you have told no one

Trust the compass pointing you toward
Fields of tulips and the smell of new rain
And more sunshine than you've ever seen

III

You can do this without crumbling
You can do this without running back

To those familiar shadows
Where you've been hiding and where
Who you once thought you were
No longer lives

She took off for the light a long time ago
While you were too busy feeling sorry
For yourself and responsible for
Everyone else's shattered feelings
Don't you see her waiting for you up ahead?
Her hand is out and yes, Honey --
She's reaching for you and yes, it's time to go

Only a Little While

You don't want to think
About them leaving
But the day always comes
Much sooner than arriving

And their hugs like fists
Squeeze your heart
Until it explodes into
Shards of all that time passed

And how could
All that time be gone so fast

You have no choice but
To let them go back to
Their lives as you return
To yours and you thank them

For including you in theirs
For a little while because
As you let them go you remember
It's always for only a little while

Until they come back again
And you can breathe easy
Because they always
Always come back again

A Certain Kind of Sadness

you want guarantees
where there are none
matters of the heart
don't come with
a gold seal
promising 100% satisfaction
or your money back

in matters of the heart
you don't get
your money or
your time back
no *shipping's on us*
and here's your return code

what you do get, though
is a lifetime of memories
filled with moments
that shatter your soul
in that good way,
in the best possible way

a certain kind of sadness
and that —
that has to be
worth something
at the end of it all

At Last Alive

And then the snow comes
Rendering air and thoughts
Silent under cotton twilight

In the absence of sound
Your world goes soft and
You taste your childhood

The purple cold outside
Takes you to the hill where
You sliced open one eye

A collision with ice and
The boy you liked and
You didn't cry because

You felt too alive
On that hill in the snow
With the boy and the ice

Down the hill again
and again with him
By your side

Snow in your boots
Fingers frozen like the
Trees and power lines

The scar has faded and
If you're lucky you can
Feel it there above your eye

And taste the cold and
Purple twilight and smell
New snow at last alive

Homecoming

I'm looking at the sky
Through a patch of Queen Anne's Lace
Growing wild along the shore

July's Silhouette
Gilded clouds float above Blueberry Hill
And the lake is on fire with the sunset

This is almost as good as sex
Almost as heavenly as his body next to mine
The sound of him breathing

The music of sleeping with someone you love
My heart is full here, brimming with golden light
The lungs of this place expand and release

And I move gently through each day
Into each good night whose chiseled arms
Are almost as strong as his

A kind and loving darkness
Exploding with stars folding into myself
Welcoming me home again

Flint

A rock tells how it is
Solitary flecks of flint
Flashing in lowered light
Geological fireflies
Pointing you forward
In the dark

Promises whispered when
You weren't paying attention
In your absent-mindedness
Hills wore themselves down
From mountains
Rounded and soft
Like an old man's shoulders

You put your tongue against
The granite where water
Runs lonely and cold
Not even starlight
Finds its way there

That's how it feels
In the shadows of trees
With trunks too big
To wrap your arms around
Fire will find its way home
Down that mountainside and
You'll be long ago gone

Rafting Up

And then there were loons
Six of them
Rafting up near the buoys
Untethered and connected
Bobbing on the wake
I watched the waves crest
And their snowy breasts
Moved with the rhythm of
An ancient gentle song

And then I dove into the lake
Dark like the growing sky
Over Blueberry Hill
Dark like my heart
Full as it was with doubt
And the fear of

Not being enough
Not knowing enough
Not giving enough
Never good enough

For the men
I handed my heart
They didn't ask and
Their waters were too deep
Their shores too sharp and steep
For even me to traverse
Without falling and feeling
That tragic undeniable sting

And then there were loons
Six of them

Bobbing and fishing
On the gentle lake
Connected and untethered
Their dark heads
A gift reminding me that
There's always enough and
I am enough
I am enough
Yes, I am enough

Swimming on What Would Have Been Your Dad's 85th Birthday

Wide angle lens on the lake
The perfect shot

Water sparkling in late afternoon sun
Trees heavy with cones
The sky his favorite shade of blue
And bluer than any sky should be allowed to be

Wind blows hard from the Northwest
As you swim into the spray of
Whitecaps like teeth
Cutting across the water

Looking back toward the dock
You see only one head bobbing
Where there used to be two
Still, your mom is smiling because she remembers

He would have gone sailing today
He would have swum with us
He would have looked up at the trees
And the sky and the sun sparkling

Like diamonds on the waves and said,
"Dear Ones, this is exactly my kind of day."

Rescue

I can't save you
From yourself

I can only show you
That it's possible

To save yourself
For yourself

And live the life
You've always dreamed of

Because you chose and
Because you could

Unbound

what if the secret
to a long
and robust life

to happiness

to joy

to the unbridled
anticipation of love

and love

and love love love

can be found
unbound
from expectation

alive

along the edges
in the willingness
and the wilderness
to go on

betting it all on
getting it all
more or less
wrong

more or less
all the time

and what if
getting it wrong
more or less
all the time
means

getting it right
in the only way
getting it right
means anything
at all

would it make
the fight

for love

and love

and love love love

more or less
all the time

worth the tears
and the scars
and wishing
on stars

alone
in your knowing

together
in owning

your gorgeous
glorious solitude

You can do good things for yourself

Don't wait too long
To feel so good
Begin now
Give yourself
The gift of

Movement
Kindness
Belief
Love

You can do
Good things for yourself
Starting today
This second
Now

Don't wait for
Someone else
To hand you
A permission slip
To say it's okay

Bust forward fast
Into the outstretched arms
Of what you
Most want to feel

The embrace of
Taking your
First deep breath
Because you said

It's time
I can
Yes

Love Anyway

Life will break you
Love anyway

People will disappoint you
Believe in them anyway

You weren't meant to travel
Unscathed, unscarred

Fully intact
That's not how this works

The world will put a hammer
To your fragile heart

Wrap its meaty paws
Around your tender throat

Punch a bloody fist into
Your pretty mouth

Slam your body to
The hard cold ground

And you will break
You will break

And you won't want
To get back up

And you won't want
To forgive or forget

And you won't want
To turn the other cheek

Or gather up the pieces
Of your shattered dignity

And keep on walking
Head held high

Walk onward, dear one
Walk onward in your light

Yes, life will break you
And you can still love

You can still live and
Love anyway

Migration

How do the geese know
When to fly to the sun?

Who tells them the seasons
And makes clear the reasons?

When the red squirrels scamper
And dig fast in the ground

Do they sense in their bones
The scent of the snow?

Why do wild horses
And elephants run?

What tips the beaver
Its lodge is done?

How do I know when
It's time to move on?

Flight

You will know when
It's time
To take your life
Out of second gear
Feel the wind again
In your face and
Through your hair
Fly down the road
Into who you are now
And who you are
Becoming

Gulf

What's hard
Is knowing
In the end
I'll be okay
Without you

The River Only Runs One Way

At one time
>This was the music

And that man
>Loved that woman

And they both believed
>In the sound and

The way
>Their mouths moved

Smooth across stones
>And forever along

The gentle slope
>Of the songs

Acknowledgments

No book is possible without a squad of dedicated people who lend their talents and gifts to the project.

And no poet is possible without an audience who appreciates this ancient, universal form of expression. Thank you, dear reader, for choosing to add this book to your personal library.

A special note of appreciation for RM -- thank you for inviting me into your world and taking me to the stars.

Extra hugs and gratitude to independent bookstores everywhere and the following people who believe in me, who support art in all its variations including poetry, who do great work, and who show up to life with humor, love, kindness, generosity, and grace.

Melissa Bauer, Amy Bobchek, Margaret Bowles, Tommy Breedlove, Val Castillou, Sharon Castlen, Renee Cunnigham, Lawrence Fielden, Peter and Sara Glavin, Jen Griffin, Geri Ann Higgins, Kirk Hoessle, Tracy Imm, Sharon Jeffe, Ben Kayser, Ginna Kayser, DJ King, Diane Law, Jill Lopez, Mary Grace Lyman, the entire Lyman Family, Chris Miller, Erika Moore, Jane Moore, Kathy Mullen, Shannon Mulroy, Susan Perry, Lisa Ripi, Diana Rosinus, Leta Russell, Renee Simas, Angela Talbott, Alice Tang, Vinod Thomas, and Dr. Douglas Wright, Alyssa & Melissa -- you each hold my heart.

Finally, Dad -- you brought me to the water and taught me it's a hard place to beat. You may be gone, but I imagine you up there still messing about in boats.

About the Author

Mary Lou Kayser is a pioneering author and speaker at the forefront of the intersection between poetry and personal transformation. Her work is celebrated for its ability to facilitate profound personal journeys, making her a leading figure in the emerging category of transformative literature.

Mary Lou is a dedicated writer, speaker, podcaster, and educator, weaving together the intricate threads of leadership and self-discovery. She continues to leave an indelible mark as a teacher, online business owner, workshop leader, copywriter, and confidante to business leaders seeking to amplify their voice. adventure and creativity.

Throughout her illustrious career, she has embarked on diverse adventures, from guiding white water rafting expeditions in Alaska to nurturing the growth of budding entrepreneurs. Whether kayaking through serene waters, indulging in wine tasting escapades, or immersing herself in the tranquility of the woods, she finds inspiration in every facet of life.

Mary Lou divides her time between Oregon and New York, with side trips to Maine whenever she can. To learn more about Mary Lou Kayser and invite her to your next event, visit www.MaryLouKayser.com